Minimalism

How to Minimize Your Monthly Expenses

Colvin Tonya Nyakundi

Simple Life Books

JD-Biz Publishing

Check out some of the other Entrepreneur Series books
Entrepreneur Series books on Amazon
Check out some of the Science of Living Series books
Science of Living Series on Amazon
Check out some of the Health Learning Series books
Health Learning Series on Amazon

Table of Contents

Expert Advice on How to Minimize Your Monthly Expenses

Introduction

An average family in the United States earns about $50,000 annually. That figure translates to slightly more than $4,000 each month. With the ever increasing prices of basic commodities and the high cost of living, it is quite important that you learn how to minimize your monthly expenditure. Regardless of the amount of money you earn, you have to save as much cash as possible so as to safeguard your future.

It is very unfortunate that some people have poor money management skills to the extent that they exhaust their income before the end of the month. Such people end up having huge debts and may be forced to sell some of their property in future. Some of the factors that determine the amount of cash you spend include your lifestyle, membership to clubs and living conditions.

Do you know that you can save so much cash by simply reducing the money you spend on paying professional cleaners and gardeners? Why don't you do the job whenever you have the time to do it?

The book "Expert Advice on How to Minimize Your Monthly Expenses" is designed to help you know what to do and what not to do so as to save as much money as possible. After reading this book, you'll know how you can minimize the money you use for meals, travelling to/from work, apparel, entertainment, utility bills, school fees and medical expenses.

Enjoy reading the book "Expert Advice on How to Minimize Your Monthly Expenses!!!"

Minimizing Money Used For Utility Bills

So as to minimize your monthly expenditure on utility bills, you should never leave tap water running for no reason. Some people have the habit of living water running for several minutes while they are attending to other issues. You should open the tap only if you're going to use the water there and then.

(repair leaking taps and water pipes)

You must also nurture the habit of repairing leaking water pipes as soon as possible. Even when you think that that the rate of water leakage is quite low, the fact is that you're the one who will pay the bill. Why pay more when you can reduce the bill by simply fixing the pipe?

You can also reduce your monthly expenditure by harvesting rain water. Just build a tank and a gutter that collects rain water from the roof before feeding it to the tank. The cost of constructing a concrete water tank or buying a plastic one might be high but you'll end up saving more money in the long run.

Apart from harvesting rain water, you can also drill a borehole in your compound. A borehole is quite expensive to drill, but you'll save a lot of money if you consume so much water each month. If you live near a river, it will be cheaper to purchase a water pump and use it to pump water from the river to your home.

When using alternative sources of water, it is quite important to ensure that the water is safe before consumption. You should therefore treat the water before it is used in your home. Alternatively, you can decide to use water from utility providers for consumption (drinking, cooking and cleaning dishes) and water from other sources for other purposes such as irrigation. Just make sure that the plumbing network in your home is well designed so that water from different sources doesn't come into contact with each other.

You should also learn the culture of recycling water in your home. For instance, you can clean the verandah using the water that you used in rinsing laundry. The same water can be used to clean your car.

Apart from reducing the money used for water bill, you should also reduce your monthly expenditure on electricity. In an average American home, electricity bill takes a huge portion of the money used for utility bills each month.

When purchasing electronic gadgets such as TVs, subwoofers and radios, you must consider the power rating and efficiency of the gadgets. All these details are available on the gadget's nameplate which is normally placed at the back of the gadget or in the user manual. The efficiency of the gadget indicates the percentage of power lost when the gadget is on. On the other hand, the power rating indicates the total amount of power consumed by the gadget per unit time. Always ensure that you go for a gadget with high efficiency and lower power consumption. Even if the gadget might be expensive than other gadgets, you'll end up saving more money in the long run.

(unplug electronic devices instead of using a remote or the power button to turn them off)

You should never leave any electronic gadget on when not in use. Even if the gadget consumes very little power you should switch it off and unplug it from the socket. Don't just switch an electronic gadget off using the remote controller-ensure that you've unplugged it from the power source. This is because all electronic gadgets consume some power for as long as they are connected to a power source.

Before going to sleep, go round the house and make sure that all sockets are switched off.

Ensure that you laptop and/or desktop computer is well maintained and blown to remove dust. Poorly maintained gadgets consume more power than well maintained ones. For instance, a poorly maintained desktop or laptop starts overheating as soon as it is turned on. The computer's fan therefore turns on immediately and starts drawing more power.

With the extremely high environmental temperatures during summers, most families can't afford to do without fans. However, do you know that you can save so much money by simply opening the windows instead of always turning on the fans? Opening windows is highly encouraged in windy areas and in homes facing the ocean and other large waterfronts.

You could also be spending more money on electricity bill because of a fault in the wiring in your home. With improper grounding, electric gadgets overheat and hence consume more power. So as to reduce your expenditure on electricity, you should hire a qualified electrical engineer to do the wiring in your home.

While installing the lighting system in your home, ensure that you use energy saving bulbs such as those made from light emitting diodes (LEDs). In order to produce the same amount of light (luminance,) LEDs consume significantly less power than regular bulbs such as incandescent lamps. One more advantage of LED lamps is that they have a longer lifespan. Apart from using energy saving bulbs, you must also limit the number of bulbs i.e. you should get rid of all the extra/unnecessary lambs in your home.

Even though the installation cost is high, solar water heaters save a lot of money for an average American family. Instead of heating water using electricity, try using solar water heaters and you'll be surprised at how much you'll save that month.

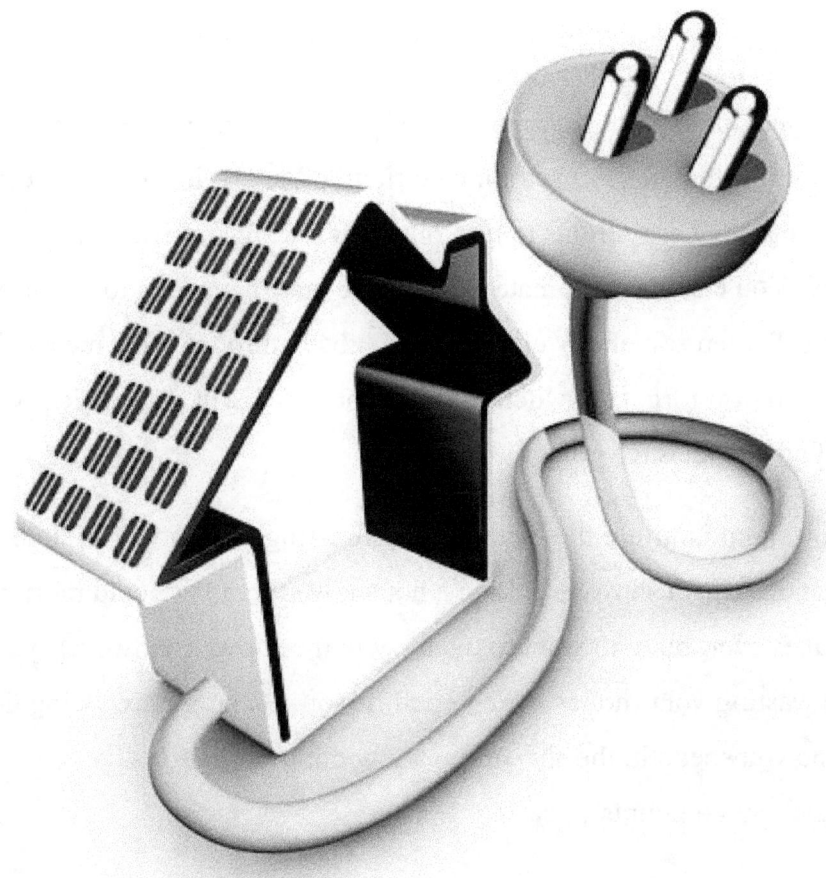

(install a windmill instead of relying on power from utility service providers)

Instead of relying on electric power from your utility service provider you should try installing your own power source. One of the best forms of energy is renewable energy such as wind and solar. You can save so much cash by simply installing a windmill or solar panel.

If your home is located near a river, you can install your own hydro-generator to supply power to your home. Keep in mind that when generating your own electricity, you can sell the surplus power to your neighbors and get some extra cash in the process.

Automating electric equipment in your home can also help you minimize the money used for electricity bills. For instance you can automate security lights to turn on or off during specific times of the day. You can also automate the bulbs in your bathroom to be turning on/off when somebody enters or exits the bathroom. This means that even if you forget to switch off the lights, they will automatically turn off and hence save power.

You should nurture the culture of minimizing the amount of time you spend taking a shower. Taking a hot shower on a very cold morning makes everybody to want to overstay in the shower. However, you'll be wasting your money for no good reason. By simply reducing the time you spend in the shower by a few minutes, you'll save significant amounts of cash.

Three phase electrical loads (such as motors) consume a lot of electrical power when operating under poor power factor. You should therefore ensure that they are operating on high power factor. When installing such loads, you should consult an electrical engineer to help you improve the power factor.

In distribution of electricity, the amount of energy lost in the system is directly proportional to the length of the cables. You should therefore never-over extend electrical cables without consulting an electrician. However, when installing electric gadgets within your home, you shouldn't worry about extending electric cables. The amount of energy that is lost during distribution of power over short distances is insignificant.

Limit the number of premium cable TV channels that you're subscribed to. After all, how many hours do you spend in your home each day? Why subscribe to so many channels when you know very well that you won't ever watch most of these channels.

Minimizing Your Monthly Transportation Expenditure

If you're keen on minimizing your monthly expenditure, you must start thinking of ways to reduce the amount of money you spend travelling to and from work each day. You must also find ways to reduce the money you use when visiting long distance and nearby relatives.

(ensure your car is well maintained)

So as to reduce your expenditure on transportation, you must ensure that your car is well maintained. This is because well maintained automobiles consume much less fuel than poorly maintained ones. For instance, the wheel air pressure affects the amount of fuel consumed by the car. You should therefore seek professional advice on how to optimize wheel pressure for optimal car performance.

Instead of always relying on your mechanic to fix your car, you should learn the basics of car repair. Mechanics charge so much money to fix small problems such as changing a wheel after a flat tire. Some people don't even know how to add water to the engine or battery. Such basic tasks should be done at home. Don't wait until your car breaks down before you start running up and down in search of the nearest mechanic. Learn something about your car and how to repair simple problems.

How many cars do you own currently? Instead of owning several cars that you rarely drive, why not sell some of them? By simply selling some of the cars that you own, you can save on the insurance money. You should also never buy more cars than your family needs. If your household comprises of four members, you should never have more than four cars at any given moment.

You should also consider selling your current automobile and investing in one with a smaller engine capacity. When driving a car with a smaller engine capacity, you'll reduce your monthly expenditure because such cars consume significantly less gas. You can also reduce fuel consumption by purchasing a hybrid car.

(consider sharing a car with your spouse or neighbors to work)

You can also minimize your monthly expenditure by sharing a car with your wife or neighbors whenever going to/from work. This is applicable in cases where you work in the same workplace or your workplaces are near each other.

Instead of always using your car to get to work, you should consider using public means of transportation such as a bus or train. When compared to using your own car, travelling to work using public means of transportation is quite cheap.

If you're keen on minimizing your monthly expenditure, you must never drive your car for abnormally long distances. Apart from the high fuel consumption, you risk causing an accident due to fatigue. You'll also be wasting so much time. Instead of driving your car for long distances, you should use a train or fly to your destination and then hire a car for the small period of time that you'll be there.

You can also minimize your monthly expenditure by limiting the number of times you visit a long distant relative or friend. However, this doesn't mean that you shouldn't visit them at all.

If your company provides cars for its employees, you should consider requesting to be allocated one. Even if you don't like the type of cars allocated to employees in your company, the fact is that you'll save some money by using that car.

You don't have to drive to the shopping mall or country club if it's right next to your home. Instead of always depending on your car to get to nearby places, you should nurture the culture of walking. When thinking of shopping during weekends, holidays or when you're too idle, you should consider walking to the shopping mall instead of driving there.

(drop your kids at school instead of hiring somebody else to do it)

Instead of hiring a driver and using a separate car to drop your children at school, you can drop them there while on your way to your workplace. This way you'll save the money that you could have paid the driver, insured the other car and fueled it.

Instead of selling your car and then buying a new one, why don't you continue using it for the time being? By frequently selling and buying cars, you'll be spending more money than you could have spent when using just one car. Replace your car when it is absolutely necessary to do so.

You must always ensure that your car has comprehensive insurance cover. You never know what is going to happen once you hit the road. Rather than risk spending your money repairing a car that has been involved in an accident, why don't you insure it?

Automobiles consume more gas when being driven slowly. This means that you should avoid traffic jams if you're keen on minimizing your monthly expenditure. You can beat traffic jams by waking up very early in the morning and driving to work before other commuters get on the road.

Before settling on any particular gas station, you must ensure that it is the cheapest and best gas station in town. However, this doesn't mean that you should waste your time (and fuel) going from one filling station to another until you find the cheapest one. You need to do that for the first time only. After you've identified the best filling station, stick to it and be a loyal customer. You should also ensure that the gas station sells pure gasoline. Remember that impure gasoline reduces a car's performance and lifespan.

In order to minimize your monthly expenses, you should plan your day properly so as to accomplish several tasks at the same time. For example, when coming from work in the evening, you can pass by the grocer to buy vegetables, then go to pick your kid from school before heading home. Don't go home then go back to the grocer then home then to pick your kid at school.

Minimizing Your Monthly Expenditure on Meals and drinks

Whether you believe it or not, meals and drinks account for a very huge portion of your total monthly expenditure. The money is spent on breakfast, lunch and dinner. This means that when thinking of minimizing your monthly expenses, you must start thinking of how you can reduce your expenditure on meals and drinks.

(invest in a sizeable refrigerator)

So as to minimize your monthly expenditure, you should invest in a highly efficient refrigerator. The refrigerator will allow you to buy perishable meals (e.g. milk and vegetables) in bulk without having to worry about them going bad. Apart from just purchasing a refrigerator, you should never buy more perishable meals than can fit in the refrigerator. This is because the meals will probably get bad and waste your money in the process.

You should buy nonperishable meals (such as sugar, eggs and wheat flour) in bulk so as to benefit from economies of scale. For instance, you can decide to buy four trays of eggs at the beginning of the month instead of buying a tray each week.

You can also minimize your monthly expenditure by growing vegetables and fruits in your backyard. You'll save all the money that you spend at the grocer purchasing horticultural products such as cabbages, cucumbers, tomatoes, pepper, oranges, grapes and apples. If your house seats on a huge piece of land, you should consider keeping farm animals and birds including cows, goats and chicken. Rather than buy milk daily, why don't you keep dairy cows if you own a big piece of land? Keep in mind that you can earn some money in the process by selling the extra milk.

In your quest to minimize your monthly expenditure, you should work on your eating patterns. You should not over eat or drink. Apart from the health risks involved in overeating, you'll also be wasting money. This also means that you should not buy meals that you had not planned for. For instance, you shouldn't buy sweets and chocolates simply because you saw them on display at the mall. When going shopping for foodstuff create a shopping list and ensure that you adhere to the shopping list.

(Carry your lunch to the office)

You can also save significant amounts of cash by carrying food from your home to your workplace instead of eating in a hotel or canteen. During lunchtime, you should avoid eating packed meals from fast food outlets. If your company provides meals, you should eat the meals together with your fellow employees instead of buying meals elsewhere.

Before you start cooking any meal, you must consider the number of people expected to eat that meal. Why would you prepare a meal for four people while there are two of you in your home? Don't cook too much food as you'll end up throwing away most of it.

Instead of going out for drinks with friends, you should consider buying drinks and then drinking them at home. Nightclubs and other entertainment joints normally charge more money than what the drinks are worth. You therefore get to save money by simply drinking at home instead of going out. Remember that owners of entertainment joints are out to make profits and therefore they charge you more cash.

You can also minimize your monthly expenditure on meals by cooking instead of buying readymade food. Instead of buying dinner for the whole family from a fast food joint, you should consider cooking. Fast food joints have to charge you more cash so as to carter for employee's salaries, license from the government and profits.

Entertainment and Relaxation

An average family in the United States spends significant amounts of the monthly income on entertainment and relaxation. These expenses include the money used to fund holidays, outings, parties and dinner dates. If you're so much interested in minimizing your monthly expenditure, you should never ignore the importance of reducing your expenses on entertainment and relaxation.

(consider nearby holiday destinations)

Instead of visiting entertainment joints that are far away from your home, you should consider visiting those near your home. This way you'll get to save on transportation costs. In case you don't have a designated driver to take you back home when you're too drunk, you'll spend less money on taxi. If there is an entertainment joint in your estate, you should consider visiting it instead of going to a distant joint.

When subscribing to exclusive members clubs, ensure that you go for quality and value for money. Don't subscribe to an expensive club simply because most of your neighbors or colleagues are members there. You can go for a cheaper club, nearby and offering the same services. If possible, cancel membership to clubs that you rarely visit. Why pay thousands of dollars annually in membership fees while you rarely visit the club(s)?

Don't just wake up one day and decide to go for a trip or holiday. So as to minimize your expenses, you must always plan for trips and holidays well in advance. This will give you time to research on cheap and high quality destinations.

Instead of hosting events in hotels, or conference centers, you should consider hosting them in your home. So as to save money, you need to convert your home into a perfect venue for hosting events. You can also decide to purchase tents if you think that the number of guests will be significantly high. Whenever you're not using the tents, you can rent them and make some profit in the process.

Do you know that you can easily convert your home to the best destination for a date? Instead of taking your spouse out for an expensive dinner date, you should consider a romantic date in your own home. You'll just have to buy the drinks and meals that you could have taken at a hotel.

Together with some of your neighbors or friends, you can set up an entertainment joint or bar in your neighborhood. Instead of going elsewhere, you should go to your own bar. By drinking in your own bar, you'll be retaining all the profit. This means that you'll be minimizing your monthly expenditure.

How much money do you pay to access facilities/amenities such as swimming pools, tennis courts, saunas or gymnasiums? Instead of paying in order to access such amenities, why can't you move to a neighborhood with such facilities? So as to minimize your monthly expenditure while at the same time having fun, you can move into a neighborhood with facilities that include children playing fields, ample parking and gazebos. Your home should also be close to medical institutions, schools, malls, an airport and major highways.

When thinking of holidaying, you can save significant amounts of money by simply holidaying as a group. You can come together with a bunch of your friends, neighbors or colleagues and then organize a trip.

So as to minimize your monthly expenditure, you should avoid gambling as much as possible. Even if you think you are very lucky, the truth is that you risk so much by gambling. What if you lose all your money? How will your family survive?

Medical Expenses, School Fees, jewelry and Apparel

Jewelry, apparel, medical and school fees also consume a huge chunk of most people's income. You should therefore do something to reduce these expenses if you're keen on minimizing your monthly expenditure.

(live a healthy lifestyle)

To begin with, you must start living a healthy lifestyle. Eating healthy meals and exercising regularly increases body immunity and hence minimizing the risk of getting sick. This means that you get to save on the money that you could have used for treatment. Apart from living a healthy lifestyle, you should subscribe to a comprehensive medical insurance cover. You can also take advantage of your company's medical insurance cover.

You can also minimize your monthly expenses by going for frequent medical checkups. Some chronic diseases such as cancer can be treated if detected early enough. Instead of using so much money to treat yourself, why not go for frequent medical checkups? Remember that most insurance companies don't provide cover against such diseases.

So as to avoid the cost incurred in treating waterborne diseases, you should maintain high levels of cleanliness in your home. You must also ensure that you never consume any meal or drink that you suspect isn't clean.

Immunization can also help you reduce chances of being infected by some diseases. You must ensure that your kid is immunized from diseases such as polio and measles. Talk with your doctor for more information about the recommended types of immunization.

You must also avoid visiting countries or areas in which some diseases are prevalent. For instance, you should not visit countries in which there is Ebola outbreak or an outbreak of any other contagious disease.

So as to avoid physical injuries, you should teach your children how to play and move around the house in safety. This way you can save on the money that you could have used to treat them.

Some people spend significant amounts of money on counselors and therapists. Rather than spend your hard earned money on counselors, you should avoid stressful situations that can lead you to depression.

You can also minimize your monthly expenditure by ensuring that your kids are enrolled to a nearby school. You'll save on fuel money when visiting the school on parents' day. You should also consider the money charged by the school versus the quality of education at that school. Don't pay huge sums of money while the school is offering poor quality education.

When shopping for clothes, you should practice self-control. Don't just pick all the clothes that you like. You should also ensure that you only spend the money that you had set aside for that purpose.

(consider handing out cheaper gifts)

You can also minimize your monthly expenditure by finding better methods of celebrating your achievements. Instead of going for an expensive holiday, you can decide to visit the local zoo or museum. You should also find cheaper ways of rewarding or appreciating your partner or kid. Instead of buying a very expensive shirt, you can buy a tie or even a pair of socks. Think twice before purchasing a present for your spouse/kid. No need to buy your wife a headscarf while you know very well that she doesn't wear headscarves. There is also no reason to buy your husband a watch if he hates them. If you buy something that your spouse doesn't like, he/she will end up throwing it in the closet and it won't ever come out.

Instead of buying a new phone model, you can decide to wait for a few weeks or months before making the purchase. After being on the market for some time, most manufacturers reduce the prices of their products. You can therefore save some money by waiting for a few weeks or months before buying anything.

In order to minimize your monthly expenses, you can decide to sell the clothes that you no longer wear. Apart from saving money, you'll be de-cluttering your home. Instead of using your earnings to buy new clothes, use the money you obtain from selling your old clothes. You should also never purchase a piece of clothing that you know very well you'll never wear.

Don't keep on buying new jewelry while you never use the one that you already have. Sell the ones you have and use the money to buy new jewelry. As soon as you feel bored with the jewelry you already have, sell them before purchasing new ones.

You can also reduce your monthly expenses by reducing the amount of money you use for grooming. Consider reducing the number of times you visit a barber or the number of times your fingers are manicured each week. You should also be cautious about the amount of money you spend on shampoos.

Conclusion

Truth be told, minimizing monthly expenditure is an uphill task that very few people can manage. However, with dedication and commitment you can manage to do it on your own. Start by creating a list of everything you spend your money on. Go ahead and try to figure out a way to reduce the money you spend on each item on the list you created. You should also never forget to create a monthly budget and sticking to it.

Before purchasing anything, always ensure that you've sampled several places so as to get the cheapest deals. Even if you're a regular customer in a given outlet, you should try a different outlet someday. You'll be surprised at the amount of money that you'll save. When visiting a mall or shopping center, you should buy what you need and not necessarily what you want. Before making any purchase, ask yourself this question; are you really gaining anything by spending your money on that particular item or service?

At the end of each day, try to count your money and make sure that you can account for all the missing cash. As soon as you've started saving some cash, open a fixed deposit account so as to save all your stash. This way you won't be tempted to squander the money.

You can also minimize your monthly expenditure by avoiding debts and loans as much as possible. Debts and loans from financial institutions attract huge interest rates and hence increase your monthly expenditure. If you're in an emergency and need some cash, talk to your friends or relatives and request them to give you an interest-free loan.

Author Bio

Colvin Tonya Nyakundi is a freelance writer and co-author of 'Expert Advice on How to minimize your monthly Expenses.' Apart from that book, he has a portfolio of several other publications accumulated in the more than two years that he has been freelancing through www.odesk.com.

He has authored several personal relationships, construction and real estate, lifestyle and travel and holiday guide publications. Other books that he has co-authored include 'How to Survive in the Woods', 'How to Start Making Money Online', 'How to Survive in a Desert', 'How to Improve Your Communication Skills,' 'Construction Guide for New Investors in Real Estate,' 'How to Make Your Backyard a Magnificent Venue for Hosting Events', 'How to Identify the Perfect Holiday Destination', "How Your Favorite Meal Could be Killing You Slowly" and 'How to Prepare and Survive in a Foreign Country.' You can get in touch with him through his official Facebook account, tonyanc@facebook.com or follow him on twitter, @tonyanc.

Check out some of the other JD-Biz Publishing books

Gardening Series on Amazon

Health Learning Series

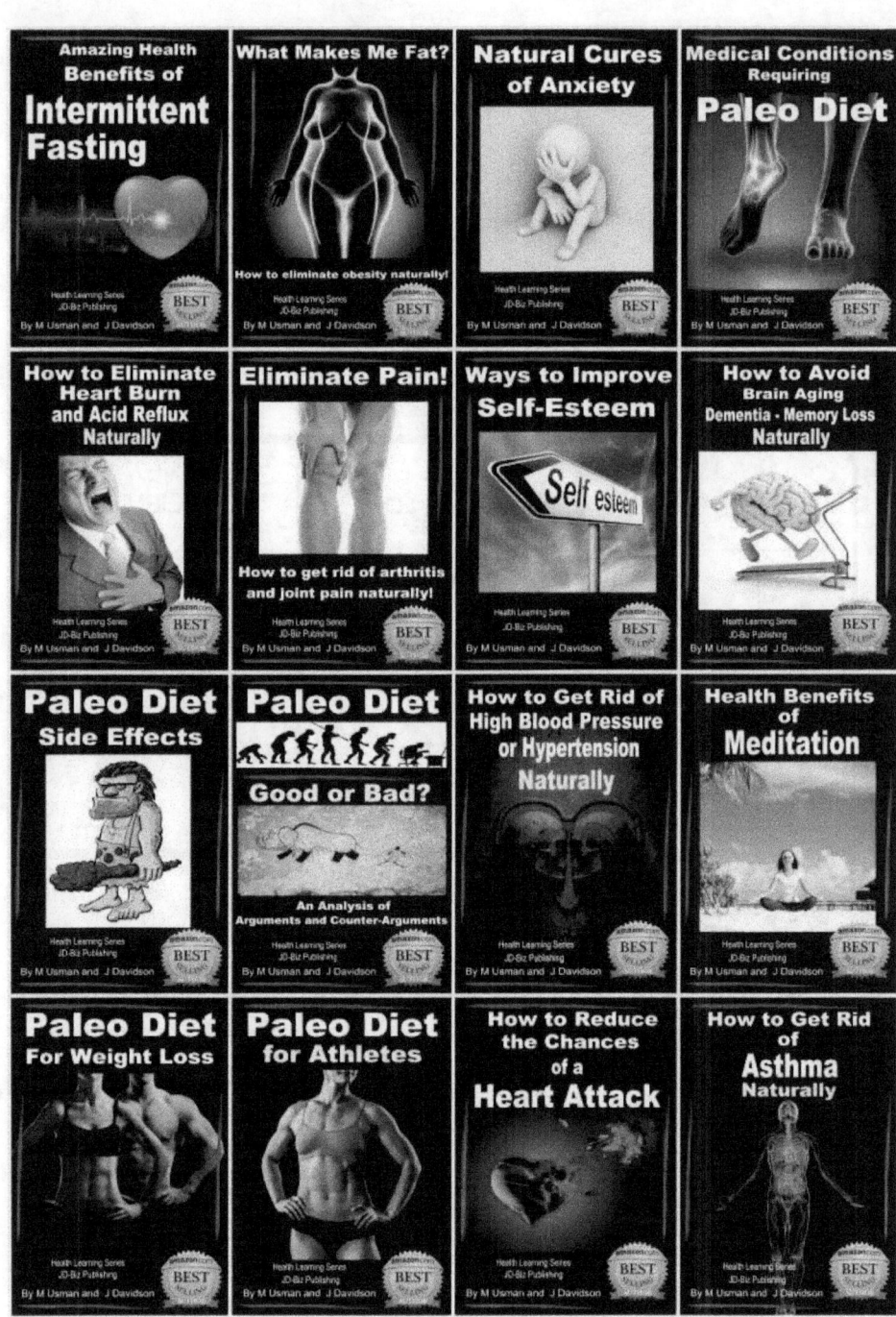

Amazing Animal Book Series

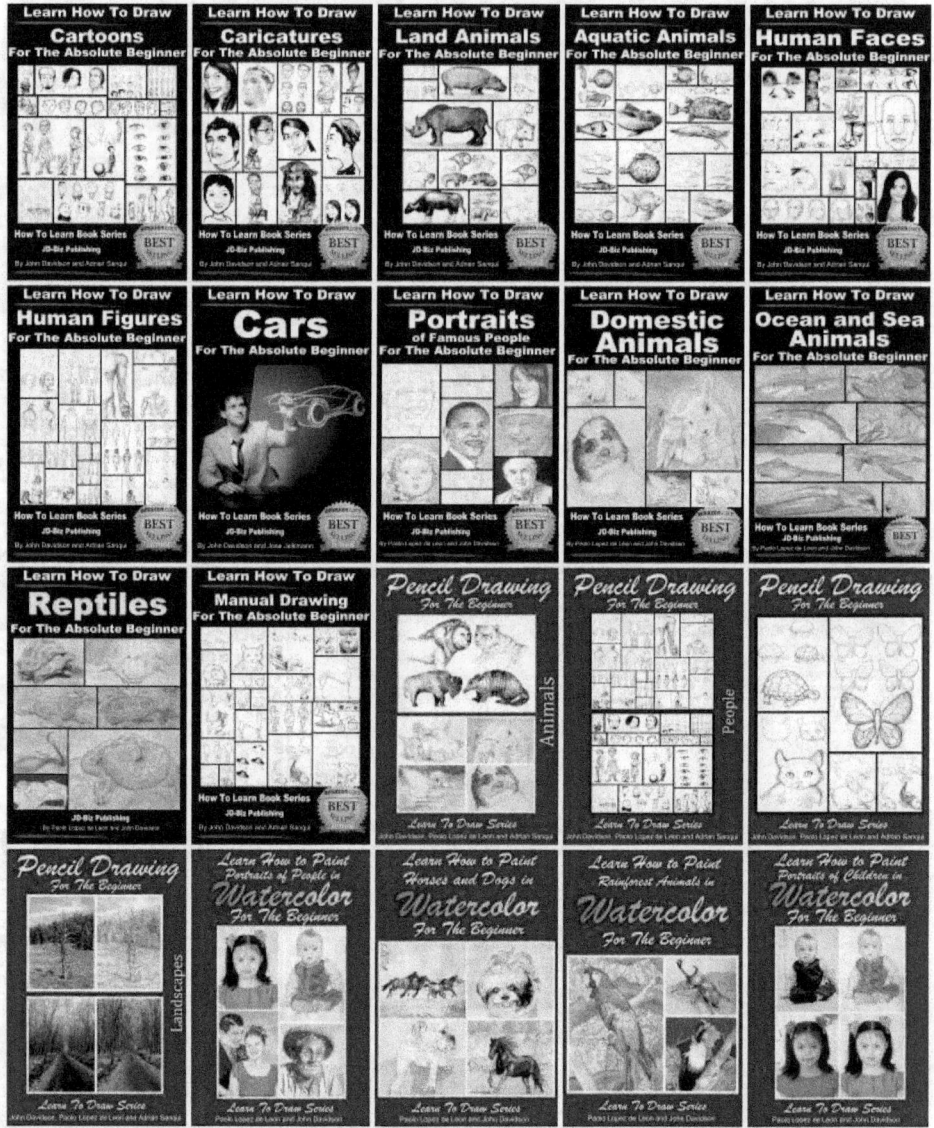

How to Build and Plan Books

Entrepreneur Book Series

Our books are available at

1. Amazon.com

2. Barnes and Noble

3. Itunes

4. Kobo

5. Smashwords

6. Google Play Books

Publisher

JD-Biz Corp

P O Box 374

Mendon, Utah 84325

http://www.jd-biz.com/

www.ingramcontent.com/pod-product-compliance
Lightning Source LLC
Chambersburg PA
CBHW071013180526
45168CB00003B/1403